Art & Activities for Kids

Draw!

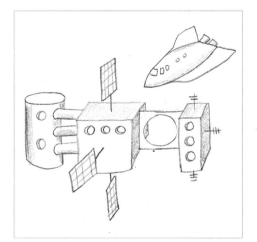

Kim Solga

NORTH LIGHT BOOKS

Cincinnati, Ohio

00 99 98 97 96   9 8 7 6 5

Library of Congress Cataloging in Publication Data

Solga, Kim.
    Draw! / Kim Solga.—1st ed.
        p.   cm.
    Summary: Encourages readers to develop drawing skills through
projects designed to teach basic principles of artistic technique and use
of materials.
        ISBN 0-89134-385-7
    1. Drawing—Technique—Juvenile literature.   [1. Drawing—
Technique.]
I. Title.
NC730.S66   1991
741.2—dc20   91-4694
                                                    CIP
                                                    AC

Edited by Julie Wesling Whaley
Designed by Clare Finney
Photography Direction by Kristi Kane Cullen
Art Production by Greg Albert and Suzanne Whitaker
Photography by Pamela Monfort
Very special thanks to Kiova Bergman, C. Griffin, Marianne Guasch,
Tami Kameda, Marissa Kimmel, Clare Lyons, Tim McEvoy, Daniel
Maczko, Stephen Nichols, Maya Small, Niki Smith, Christy Sutherlin,
Kyle G. Wesling, Jonathan Wolf, Rebecca Wolf, and the students at Sisson
School, Mt. Shasta, California.

About This Book (A Note to Grown-Ups)

Draw! features ten unique drawing projects plus numerous variations that will fire the imagination of boys and girls ages six to eleven. By inviting kids to try new things, *Draw!* encourages individual creativity. Young artists will love experimenting and developing their drawing skills while they're learning about important principles of art. Rather than drawing with only ordinary pencils and white drawing paper, they'll be encouraged to try charcoal pencils, colored pencils, felt-tip pens, crayons, pastel chalks and watercolor paints on everything from grocery bags to rolls of adding machine paper. All the while they will be learning about foreground and background, architecture and design, drawing a likeness and attention to detail, contour drawing, gesture drawing, animation, size, and drawing in 3-D.

Each project has a theme stated at the very beginning, and some projects suggest follow-up activities related to that theme. Some projects result in beautiful finished works to display or give away; others emphasize experimentation and the simple fun of *doing* them. They're all kid-tested to ensure success and inspire confidence.

Getting the Most Out of the Projects

Each project is both fun to do and educational. While the projects provide clear instructions, photographs and lots of finished examples for ideas, each is open-ended so kids may decide what *they* want to draw. Some of the projects are easy to do in a short amount of time. Others require more patience and concentration.

The materials described on pages 6 and 7 can be used for any of the projects in this book. While certain drawing tools are suggested for each project, children may enjoy experimenting with different ones. The projects are flexible to make it easy for you and your child to try as many activities as you wish. All the materials are inexpensive and are easy to find wherever school, art or office supplies are sold.

3
About This Book

6
Be a Good Artist

8
Take a Line for a Walk
Contour Drawing
Can you draw an object without ever lifting your pencil, and without looking at your paper while you draw? It's wild!

12
Animal Scribbles
Gesture Drawing
Put your pet to work as an artist's model. Even if he won't sit still, you can do quick and simple scribbles that capture the feeling and movement of your favorite animal.

16
Close-Ups
Size
Carefully draw a big picture of an everyday object. Then bring your drawing to life with tiny people climbing and working in this giant landscape.

20
Upside Down
Drawing What You See
Working from a photo, magazine, or baseball card, draw what you see—upside down! Sounds crazy, but you'll be surprised how realistic your finished drawing will look.

22
Inside Outside
Architecture and Design
Draw a house with lots of windows, from big garden doors downstairs to a tiny porthole in the tower. Cut the windows out, turn the paper over, and design the *inside* of the house!

26
Magic Tape
Foreground/Background
Use strips of tape to build a fence, then draw a flower garden all over it. Peel off the tape, and a clean, white fence magically jumps *in front of* the flowers!

28
Flip Books
Animation
You can draw a movie! Make a little book of blank pages, then draw one picture on each page. When you flip through the pages, your drawings spring to life.

32
Daring Drawing
Experiment with Tools and Techniques
Are you daring enough to try eleven drawing adventures? Tape pencils on your robot fingers, pretend your pencil has the hiccups, or try drawing with lipstick.

34
3-D Doodles
Drawing in 3-D
Learn how to make flat objects look three dimensional. Then put shapes together and add shading to make a 3-D castle, spaceport, city—anything you want!

42
My Self-Portrait
Drawing a Likeness
A self-portrait is a picture you draw of yourself as you look into a mirror. Use two mirrors to draw your profile, or make a 3-D portrait "block head."

Be a Good Artist

When you sit down to draw, what will you use?

Drawing paper. You can draw on any kind of paper, of course! Look at all the different kinds of paper the next time you're in a school or art supply store. Some paper is thick and soft, some is stiff and almost shiny. Some is really white and some is off-white or even grey. You can buy sketch pads and notebooks to keep a journal of your daily drawings.

Pencils. The "lead" in a pencil is made from graphite and clay. Some leads are soft and some are hard. Most artists like to use soft drawing pencils that make smooth, dark lines. Art pencils are marked with letters so you can tell how soft they are: "H" pencils are hard; "B" pencils are soft. The higher the number is, the harder or softer the lead is. For example, 6B is the very softest pencil. Common yellow pencils are #2, which really means 2B.

Charcoal pencils are fun to draw with, especially for making shadows because you can rub a charcoal mark with your fingertip to create different shades of grey. You can draw with charcoal sticks or fat pencils. Charcoal is made from specially burnt wood — it's *really* dark and soft.

Draw every day! Even if it's for just a few minutes at a time, if you draw every day, you'll get better and better at it.

Be warned: They're more smudgy and messy than regular pencils!

Colored pencils. You can buy a whole set of colored pencils to make color drawings. They're better than crayons for making thin lines and for coloring in small spaces. They are

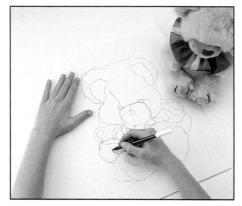

It's fun to draw from photos or use real models. It's fun to make stuff up and not look at anything while you draw. Try different ways and do what's best for you.

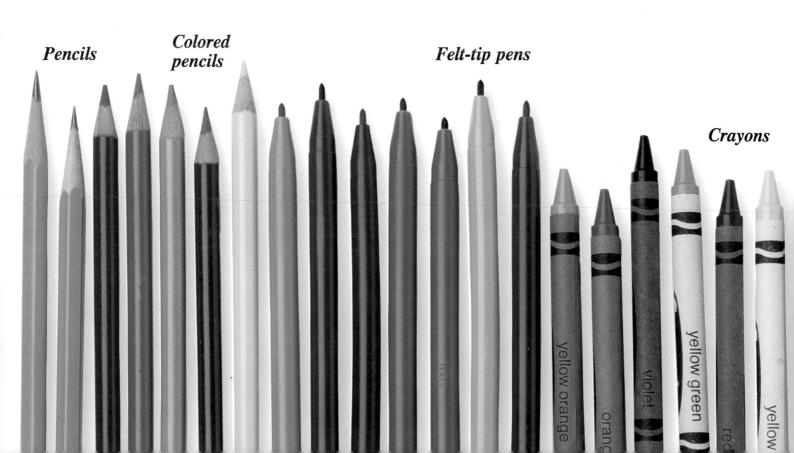

Pencils

Colored pencils

Felt-tip pens

Crayons

cleaner than markers, and the colors are lighter and easier to blend.

Crayons are good for big drawings and for coloring in big spaces. They're made of wax and come in dozens of fun colors.

Felt-tip pens or markers. Be sure to use nontoxic, water-based markers! They're great for color drawings because they make solid, dark lines. Or you can use them to put finishing touches on drawings you make with other drawing tools (like watercolors or colored pencils). If

you use more than one kind of drawing tool, it's called *mixed media*.

Chalks and pastels. Chalk creates a special effect, especially on dark paper like black or colored construction paper. It's fun to draw big pictures with chalk outside on the sidewalk or driveway! (Be sure to get permission.) Pastel chalks are messier but they come in beautiful bright colors and give your drawing a professional look.

Watercolor paint. You can draw with watercolors and a paintbrush, or use the paint to brush color on top of your pencil drawings.

Erasers. There are pink erasers and gum erasers you can use to erase guidelines and any parts of your pencil drawings you don't like. Try them both to see which you like best. The better you get at drawing, the less you'll want to erase.

You can draw with long, smooth lines or you can make lots of little wispy lines. Draw realistic pictures or make fantasy, dreamlike drawings. There's no right or wrong way to draw!

Treat your art supplies with respect. Don't put any art materials in your mouth! Always clean up your workspace and put things away when you're finished drawing.

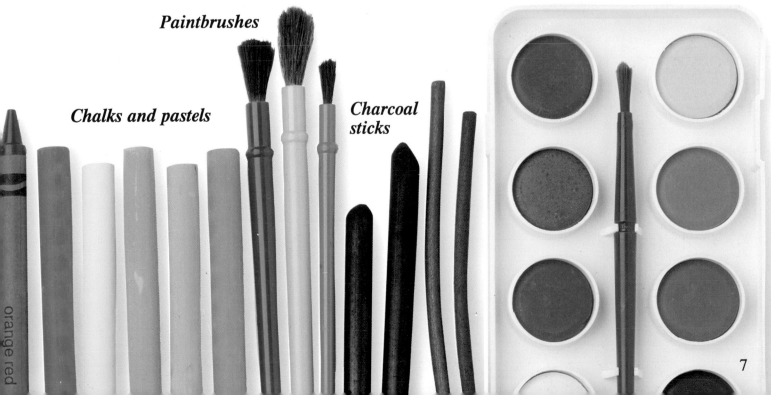

Watercolor paint

Paintbrushes

Chalks and pastels

Charcoal sticks

orange red

Take a Line for a Walk

Contour Drawing

Contour is the outline of something, especially something curvy or odd shaped. Contour drawings are fun to do because they're fast and kind of wild looking—you don't have to be very careful. The idea is to observe very closely what you're drawing and draw quickly—just the shapes you see, not the details.

Warm Up—Abstract

Make a design with one long, twisty line. Start at one corner and walk your line all over the paper. Don't lift up your pencil until your design is completely finished—fill the whole page. Try drawing only straight lines, boxes and triangles. Then try one with curls and loops and zigzags.

1 Now try a real contour drawing. Pick an everyday object like a shoe, a toy, or a plant.

2 Draw the object with one long, twisty line. *Don't look at your paper* at all—really study the object you're drawing.

3 Draw the shapes you see. Draw the lines in the object. Don't lift your pencil or pen until your drawing is all done.

When you're finished drawing, look at what you've done. It's wild and beautiful, even if it doesn't look much like the object. Try another one!

Challenge yourself to do a contour drawing of an object with many different shapes and lines.

Anything you have around the house can be the subject of a contour drawing. Try doing lots of quick sketches.

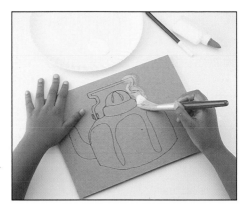

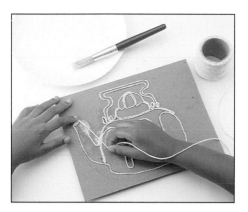

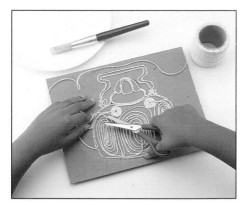

1 Now draw with one long line — of string! Sketch a picture on a piece of sturdy cardboard. Spread a thin layer of white glue all over it.

2 Stick the end of a piece of string down into the glue. Follow the lines of your sketch, pressing the string down as you go.

3 Use as much string as you can, making loops and swirls to fill in the shapes. If the glue dries, brush on some more.

Animal Scribbles

Gesture Drawings

Animals are fun to draw, but it can be hard to use a real animal as a model because they're always moving. To make realistic animal drawings, artists first make scribble drawings called *gesture drawings*. Doing gesture drawings of animals is a fast way of making sketches. All you have to do is make your scribbles look like the outline and main shapes of the animal. Don't bother with details, just scribble. Study what your animal looks like—then draw fast! It's fun to make lots of gesture drawings.

Start with an animal that's asleep. Then try doing a scribble while the animal is moving. Work fast! Your sketches don't have to be big and you can do one in less than a minute.

From Scribble to Drawing

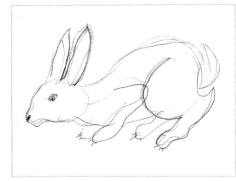

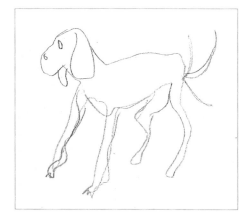

Pick one of your best scribbles to work on to make a finished drawing. Erase lines that you don't like. Draw heavier lines on top. Add eyes and whiskers; draw texture lines to show fur or feathers.

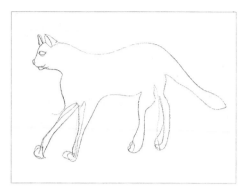

Add color or try drawing with a paintbrush and watery black paint. It's easy to make a great animal picture when you start with a scribble!

Close-Ups

Size

It's exciting to turn an everyday object—a shoe, backpack, phone or teddy bear—into an adventure scene! First make a large, detailed drawing. Then add teeny tiny people mountain climbing, skiing, horseback riding, mining coal—whatever you can think of.

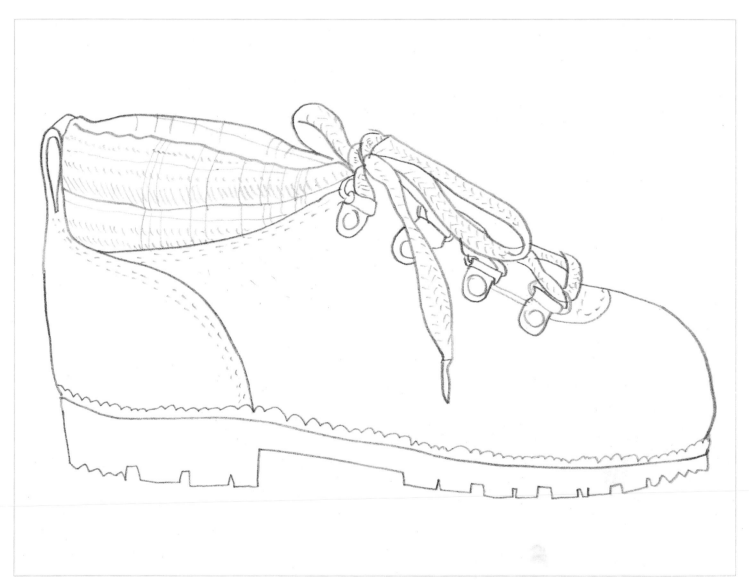

The little people will make the object you draw look huge! That's because you know how big people really are, so the object they're climbing on has to be so much bigger. This kind of size comparison is called *scale*.

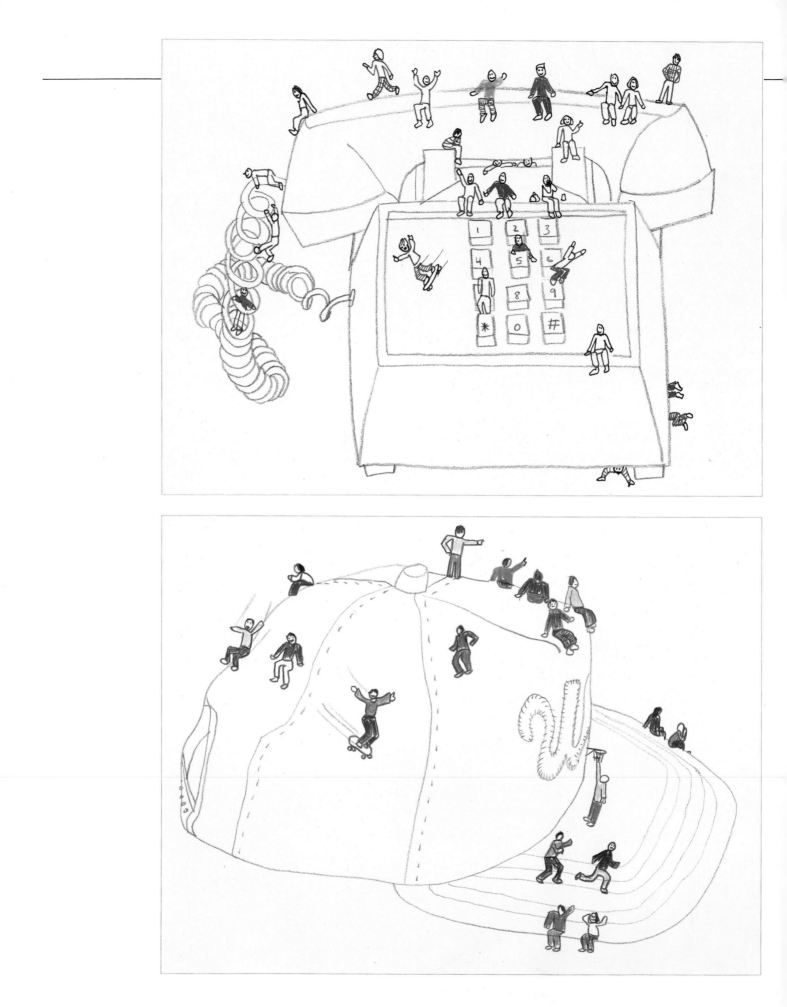

Upside Down

Drawing What You See

Drawing from an upside-down model sounds crazy, but try it and you'll be surprised how realistic your drawing will look. That's because you'll be drawing what you see, not what you think something should look like.

   Pick a photograph, a picture in a magazine, or use your favorite cartoon character. Turn the picture upside down and draw what you see. Your drawing will be upside down, too!

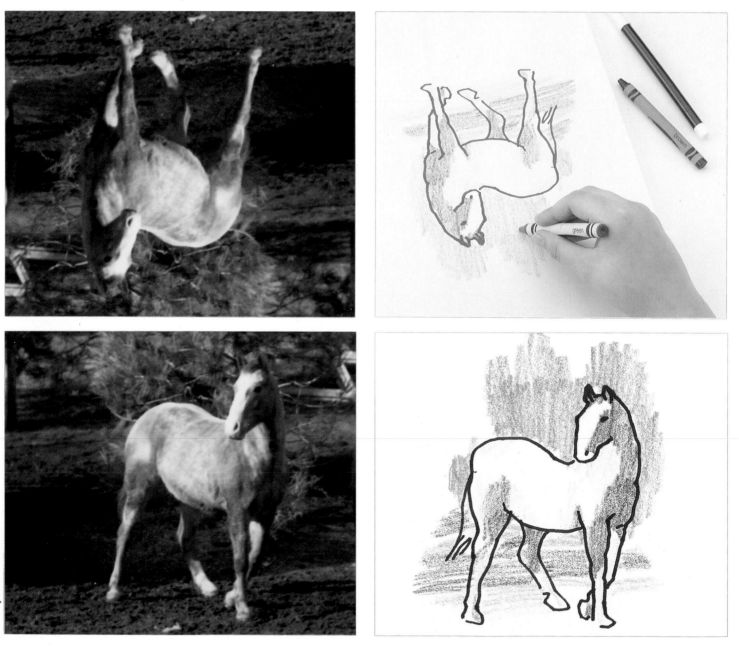

Photo by Fred W. Smith

Be careful to make the lines in your drawing match the shapes you see in the photo. Add details, always working upside down. Look at the photo closely as you draw. Erase when you need to. Turn both pictures right side up when you're finished. How does it look now?

Photo by Fred W. Smith

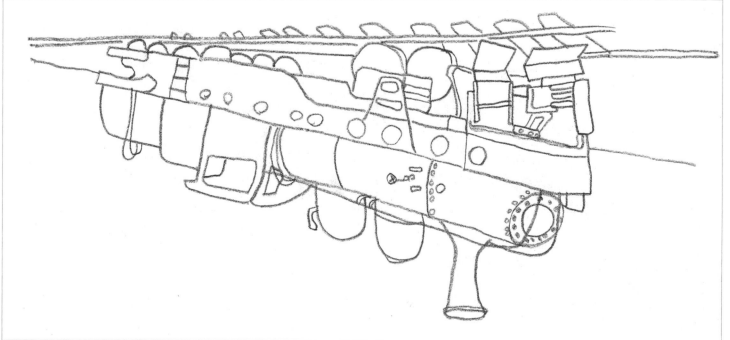

Inside Outside

Architecture and Design

If you could live anywhere you wanted, what would your house look like? Architecture is the art of making buildings. Pretend you're an architect and design your own home!

Draw the outside of your house. Make a first floor, a second floor and a roof. Add doors and windows, a garage, a greenhouse for plants, or a tower. If you run out of paper, tape another piece on and keep drawing.

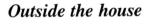

Outside the house

Cut out your house. Cut the windows out and cut the doors on three sides so they'll open. Now flip the paper over and design the inside! Plan what each room will be, and draw stairs (or an elevator), furniture, curtains and decorations.

Inside the house

My Dream House

You can create a traditional house or a silly house. Make a tall townhouse or a house shaped like a triangle. Use your imagination!

Magic Tape

Foreground/Background

These tape pictures are magic! The trick is using *drafting* tape or *removable* tape (available at office supply stores). You put the tape down and draw *over* it—your drawing is "in front of" the tape. But when you peel the tape off, the white paper jumps *in front of* your drawing! The white paper becomes the *foreground* and your drawing becomes the *background*.

Use the tape to make a fancy zoo cage. Draw an animal on top of the tape, and when you peel it off, he'll be safely behind bars.

Spell out your name with cut pieces of tape. Color bright patterns over it, then pull up the tape to see your name jump to the foreground.

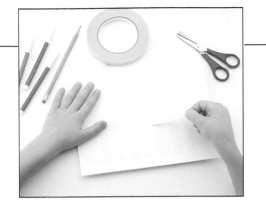  

1 Draw a line for the ground and build a fence with tape. Use it off the roll or cut some pieces down the middle.

2 Use felt-tip pens to gently draw a garden. Draw tall flowers and little flowers, thick bushes and grass. Use lots of bright colors.

3 Pull up the tape. Now the fence is in the front! You can outline it in black and draw holes and cracks to make it look like wood.

Finished garden drawing

Flip Books

Animation

You can draw a movie! *Animation* means bringing your drawings to life. First make a little book, then draw a picture on each right-hand page. Each drawing is just a bit different from the drawing before it.

The secret to making a great flip book is to press hard with your pencil to make an impression on the page *underneath* the page you're working on. Using the impression as a guide, the pictures will be in the same place on each page. Try the story ideas shown here, or make up your own.

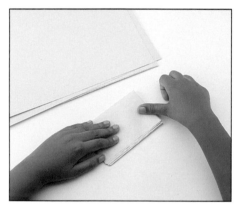

1 Fold two pieces of plain paper in half the long way. Fold them in half again across the middle, then fold them once more.

2 Unfold the last two folds and cut four sections along the fold marks. Slip these sections into each other to make a book.

3 Staple the pages together on the fold. Trim the outside edges so the pages are even.

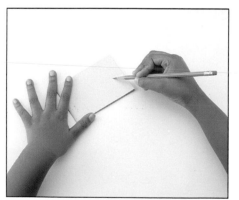

4 Start with a very simple "story": a bubble getting bigger and bigger until it pops. On the first page, draw the bubble as a tiny dot.

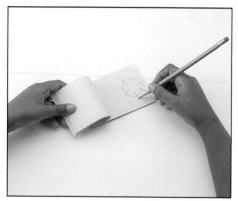

5 Draw the bubble bigger on each page. Toward the end, sketch the biggest bubble with lines bursting out from the middle.

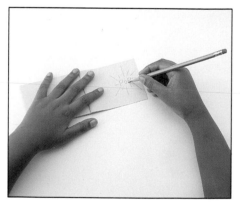

6 On the last page, draw only the bursting lines with the word "POP" right in the middle. Now try a story with more action.

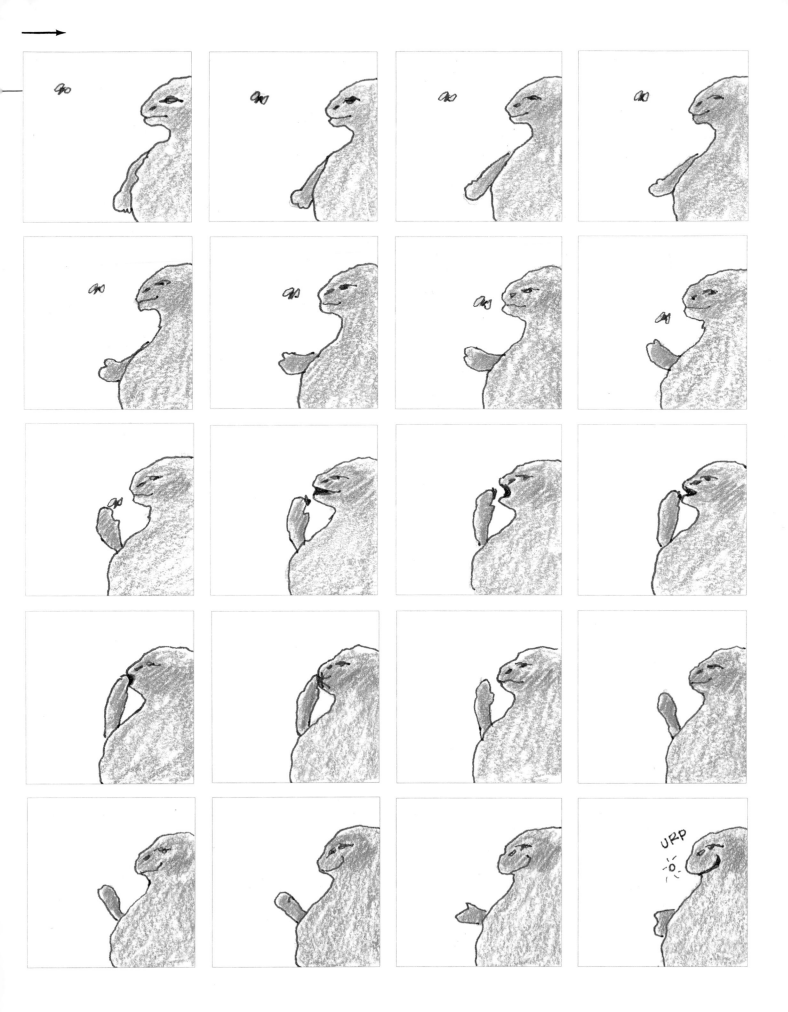

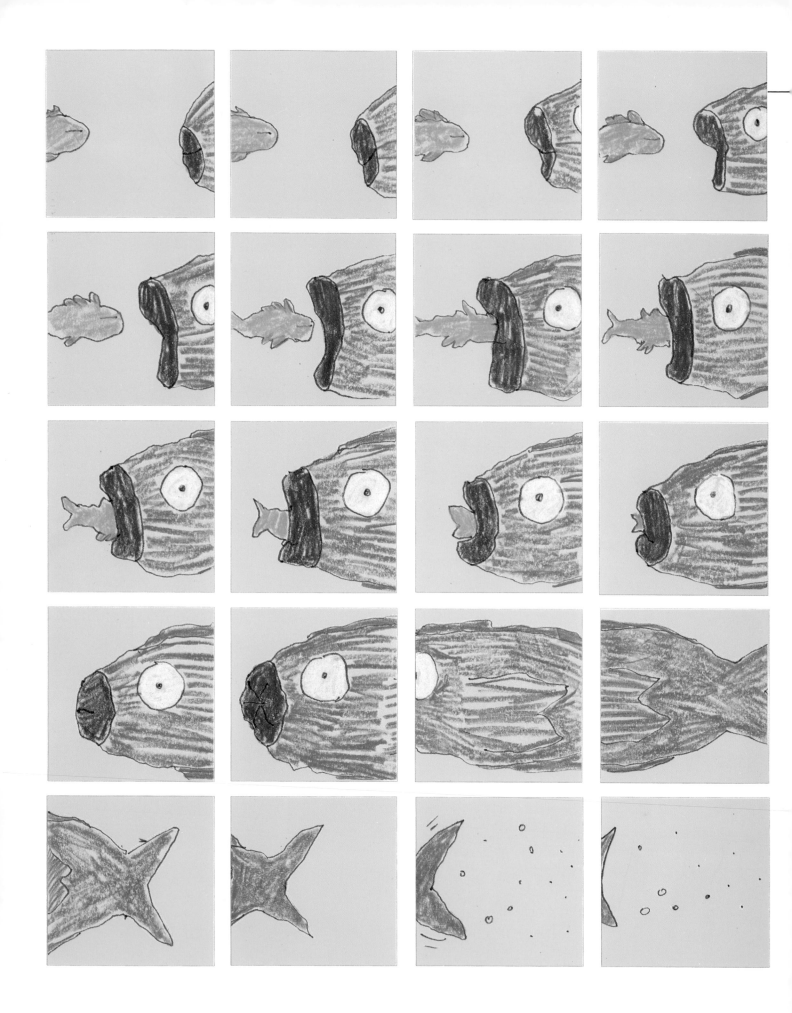

Daring Drawing

Experimenting with Tools and Techniques

Drawing doesn't have to be done with ordinary pencils on regular paper. Try drawing with light-colored pencils or chalks on dark paper. Draw with cotton-tip swabs dipped in a colored soft drink. Pretend your pencil is so heavy you can hardly lift it. Or try any of these daring drawing adventures.

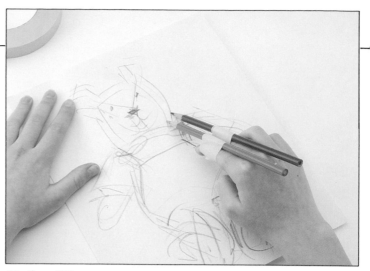

Robot Fingers. Draw with a pencil taped onto your finger, or tape colored pencils onto two fingers.

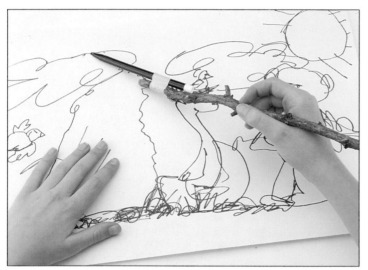

Stick with It. Tape a pencil or felt-tip pen onto a stick and draw on large pieces of paper.

Double Fun. Tape two pencils or felt-tip pens together and make a drawing with double lines.

No Peeking. Make a drawing with a towel covering your hand!

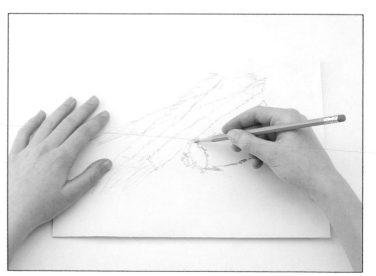

Shaky Pencil. Pretend your pencil has the jitters—or the hiccups. You can barely control it enough to draw!

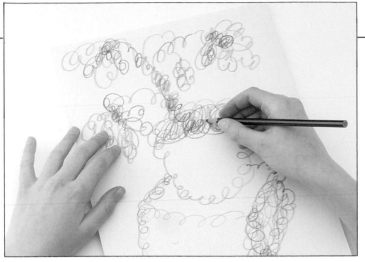

Dizzy Pencil. Pretend your pencil is so dizzy it keeps making loops and circles as you draw.

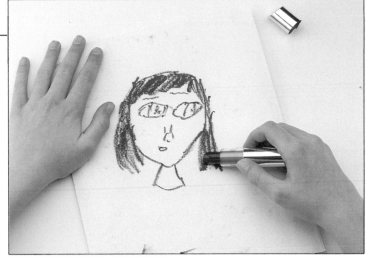

Lip-Smacking Good. Get permission to draw with an old tube of lipstick.

You're in the Driver's Seat. Make a drawing with a toy car run through paint or chalk dust.

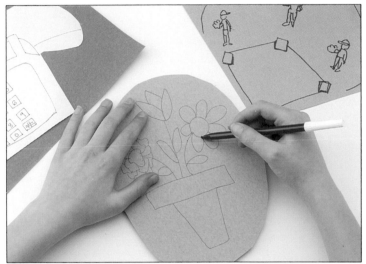

Cut Paper Drawings. Draw on construction paper cut into shapes like circles, stars and diamonds.

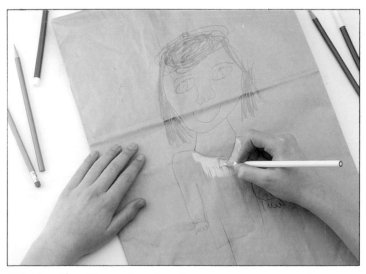

It's in the Bag. Try drawing on grocery store bags—which drawing instrument will you use?

It Adds Up. Use long rolls of adding machine paper for a long drawing or *mural*.

3-D Doodles

Drawing in 3-D

Simple drawings like stick figures look flat because they're *two dimensional*: They don't show *depth*. Being able to show depth means drawing not just the front of objects but also the sides. Drawing in 3-D is magic—you're still drawing simple lines on a flat page, but suddenly your drawings don't look flat. They look like they're jumping off the paper at you!

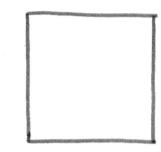  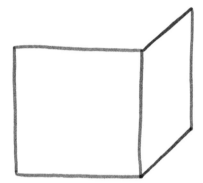

1 Draw a square.

2 Make a line like this for the back edge of the box.

3 Draw two slanted lines to finish the side.

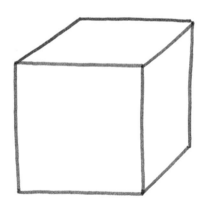 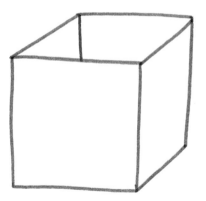 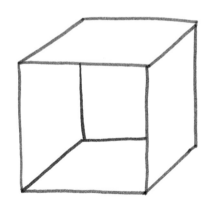

4 Finish the box top with these two lines.

5 For a box open at the top, draw a line like this.

6 For a box open in the front, draw these lines.

Box doodle.

Box open at the top.

Box open in the front.

34

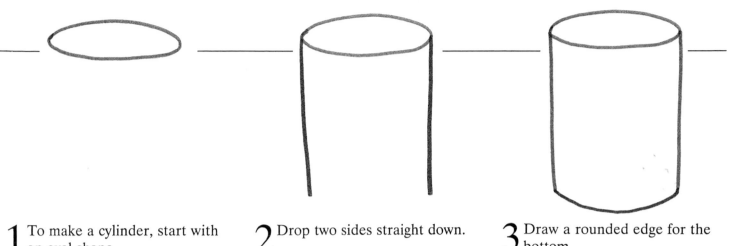

1 To make a cylinder, start with an oval shape.

2 Drop two sides straight down.

3 Draw a rounded edge for the bottom.

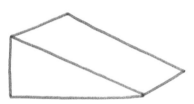

A wedge is like a thick triangle.

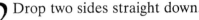
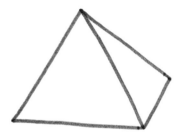

A pyramid is a 3-D triangle that comes to a point on top.

A cone is a triangle with a rounded bottom (or top).

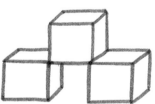
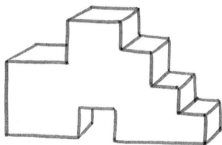
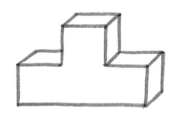

Add depth to any shape by adding lines to show the back edges and sides.

Cylinder doodle.

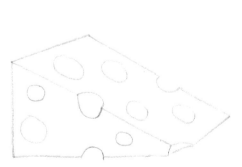

Wedge doodle.

Building doodle.

Shading Doodles

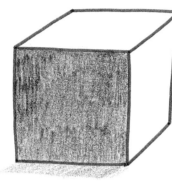

1 You can show depth by adding shading and shadows.

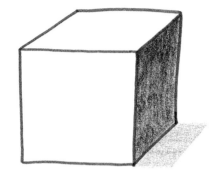

2 Pick a side to be in the shade and make that side dark.

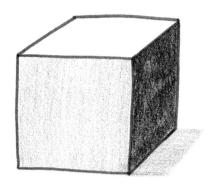

3 Add even more depth by shading another side lighter.

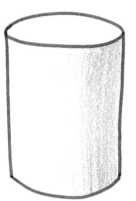

1 Shading wraps around a curved surface in a *blended tone*.

2 Make the shade dark in the back and lighter in the front.

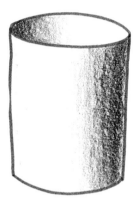

3 To make the cylinder look open, shade part of the top oval.

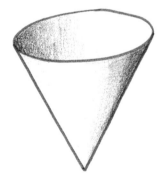

Use these rules to shade any shape.

Pick a *light source* and always shade the opposite side.

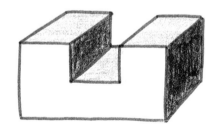

Use the same shading for all the sides that face the same way.

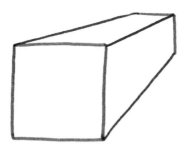
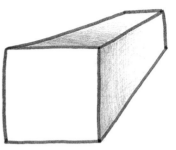

1 To make a long box, draw a big square and a tiny square.

2 Draw three long lines and erase the inside edges.

3 Add shading for a long 3-D box.

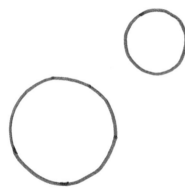

1 For a cylinder, make a big front circle and a tiny back circle.

2 Draw two long lines and erase the bottom of the back circle.

3 Shade it dark on the bottom and lighter in the middle.

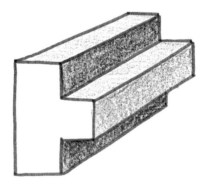
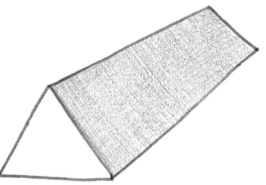

You can make any shape look long.

Remember that things look smaller the farther away they are.

So make the back end much smaller than the front end.

3-D Letters

  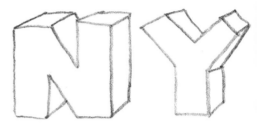

It's fun to add back edges and slanted sides to make 3-D letters.

Start with block letters that have all straight edges.

Draw lightly at first so you can erase any lines that aren't needed.

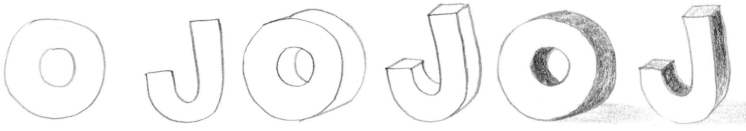

Now try making curved letters. Add shading and shadows!

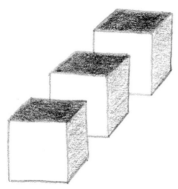 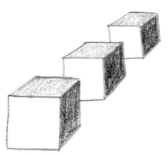 

Make things look closer or farther away by overlapping them.

Make things look even farther away by drawing them smaller.

Do the same thing with any shapes! Add shading.

 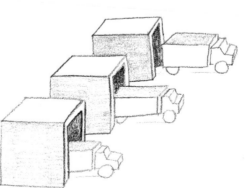 

Windows, Walls and Flags

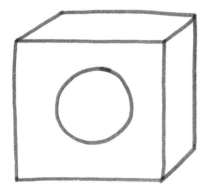

1 Create depth by showing thickness. Draw a circle on a box.

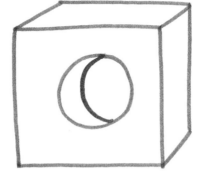

2 Draw a moon shape to make the inside edge of the circle.

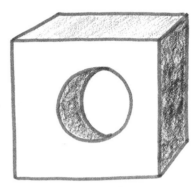

3 Add shading for a 3-D window.

Show thickness in doorways and arches the same way.

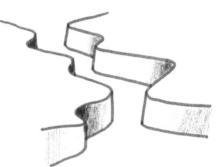

Make a wavy wall: Draw a wiggly path. Draw lines down for sides.

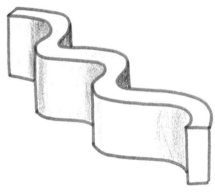

Make a bottom edge to match the top and add shading.

Use the same technique to make cliffs or flags.

3-D Drawings

You can combine shapes and techniques like overlapping, shading, and showing thickness to make wonderful 3-D drawings. Use your imagination to create realistic drawings as well as fantasy drawings. Sketch and erase, draw and shade.

My Self-Portrait

Drawing a Likeness

A self-portrait is a picture you draw of yourself as you look in a mirror. Sit in front of a mirror at a table or vanity, or use a clipboard under your paper. Study how you look in the mirror. Reach up and feel your face. What is it about your face that makes you look like you?

1 Take a close look at yourself. The front view of your head is an oval or egg shape, and your face takes up only the lower part of that shape.

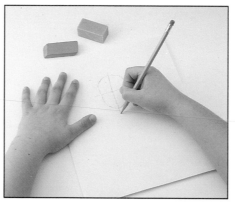

2 Draw the outside shape of your head. Make light guidelines through the middle of this shape, from top to bottom and side to side.

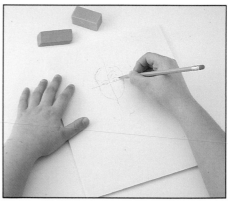

3 Sketch your eyes on the line that goes across. Above the eyes, draw your eyebrows and hair. *Look!* Your hair and forehead take more room than you think!

How much space is between your eyes and your eyebrows?

What shape is the area under your nose and above your lips?

Don't worry about making mistakes. You can always draw yourself again. The more you draw, the better you'll get at making things look real.

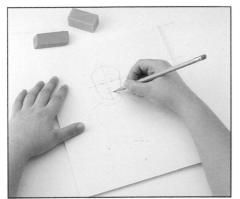

4 Below the eyes, sketch your nose, mouth and chin. Draw your ears at the same level as your nose, and your neck almost as wide as your face.

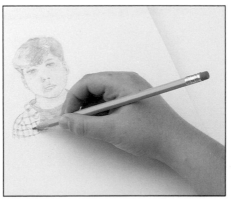

5 Erase your guidelines and draw each part of your face more carefully. Draw with smooth, strong lines. How wide is your mouth? How big are your ears?

6 Keep looking back and forth from the mirror to the drawing paper. Close one eye and measure your reflection with your fingers.

Look at Me

How do you make your self-portrait
look like *you*? Draw what you see, not
what you think you should look like.

45

My Profile

A profile is a head seen from the side. You only see one eye, one ear, one side of the nose and mouth. Have an adult help you set up two mirrors so they meet and make a corner. Sit facing one of the mirrors and you'll see your profile in the other.

Can you grin? Can you frown? Can you look angry, sad, surprised, scared or worried? Draw yourself making as many different faces as you can.

Hair is fun to draw! You can't draw every single strand of hair, so look for the edges. Draw the lines where hair meets skin, and where it curls and overlaps.

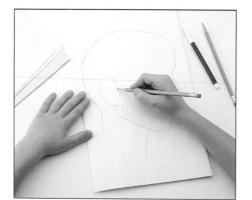

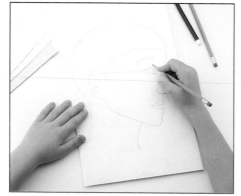

1 Take a close look—notice how much of your profile is hair! Your face takes up only part of one side. Draw the shape of your head.

2 Make light guidelines through the middle. Draw your eye on the line that goes across. It looks like a triangle with top and bottom eyelids and eyelashes.

3 Sketch the other features of your face. Then erase the guidelines and finish your drawing by adding details to your eye, nose, lips, eyebrow and hair.

Dress Up to Draw

Wear hats and scarves, jewelry and wild hairstyles when you draw yourself. Drawing costumes adds lots of fun to self-portraits.

Bright Idea

Set up a lamp beside you so that the bright light falls on one side of your face. Draw yourself and the dark shadows that the light creates on your face.

Block Heads

Once you get good at drawing your self-portrait, construct a 3-D portrait! Draw a front view of your face, a profile of each side, then fill in the top and the back (mostly hair!). Tape them together for a funny portrait sculpture.